# SEA SNAKES

## by Sneed B. Collard III
## illustrated by John Rice

BOYDS MILLS PRESS

Published by Bell Books
Boyds Mills Press, Inc.
A Highlights Company
815 Church Street
Honesdale, Pennsylvania 18431
Printed in Hong Kong

Publisher Cataloging-in Publication Data
Collard, Sneed B., III
          Sea Snakes / by Sneed B. Collard, III ; illustrated by John Rice.
—1st ed.
[32]p. : col. ill. ; cm.
Includes index, maps, photographs.
Summary : Photographs and realistic drawings illustrate the life and types of sea snakes.
Hardcover ISBN 1-56397-004-X   Paperback ISBN 1-56397-690-0
1. Sea snakes—Juvenile literature. 2. Snakes—Juvenile literature.
[1. Sea snakes. 2. Snakes.]
I. Rice, John, ill. II. Title.
597.96—dc20                     1993
Library of Congress Catalog Card Number 91-77604

First Boyds Mills Press paperback edition, 1997
Book designed by Ric Jones
The text of this book is set in 12-point Garamond.
The illustrations are done in watercolors.

10 9 8 7 6 5 4 3 2

10 9 8 7 6 5 4 3 2 1

## Dedication

*For my parents,*
*Who taught me to love all*
  *Earth's creatures,*
*And my sisters and*
  *brothers,*
*Who inspire me*
*To share that love.*
          *—Sneed*

# SEA SNAKES

## "Sea Serpents Alive and Well!"

Most of us would pay attention to a newspaper headline like this. With good reason. The term *sea serpent* conjures up tales of 50-foot snakes attacking ships and devouring sailors. We know that such monsters aren't real.

What may surprise you, though, is that different kinds of sea serpents really are alive and well. They are called sea snakes.

# SEA SNAKES

Sea snakes are not giant, people-eating monsters. Compared to land snakes like anacondas and pythons, sea snakes are quite small. Most grow no longer than three feet. The biggest ones measure about eight feet. But what is a sea snake?

**Sea krait**

**True sea snake**

Sea snakes consist of two groups—the true sea snakes and the sea kraits. All sea snakes have learned to live especially in oceans or lakes. True sea snakes live entirely at sea. There, they hunt, rest, and reproduce. True sea snakes have live babies and give birth right in the water.

# SEA SNAKES

Sea kraits also spend much of their time at sea. Unlike true sea snakes, however, they don't bear live young. Instead, sea kraits lay eggs. They come ashore to lay these eggs and to rest. Both true sea snakes and sea kraits are very venomous.

There are more sea snakes than any other kind of marine reptiles. More than fifty species live in the world's oceans. Sea snakes inhabit coral reefs, muddy mangrove swamps, salt marshes, and the mouths of rivers. Some of them even live out in the open ocean and never come close to land.

*When a sea snake bites another creature, it can inject a poison called* **venom**. *A snake that is poisonous is also called* **venomous**.

# SEA SNAKES

Sea snakes are found from along the east coast of Africa to the west coasts of North and South America. But sea snakes don't live everywhere. They live and breed only in warm, tropical and subtropical waters. And no sea snakes are found in the Atlantic Ocean. Why not?

The first sea snakes lived in the waters of Australia and Asia. But by the time the snakes began to spread out, North and South America were already connected by land.

Since sea snakes can't survive in cold water, they had no way to get around the tips of South America or Africa to the Atlantic Ocean.

*Sea snakes can't stand cold water. But they can't stand water that is* **too hot***, either. In very warm places, sea snakes may dive to deeper, cooler waters to "chill out."*

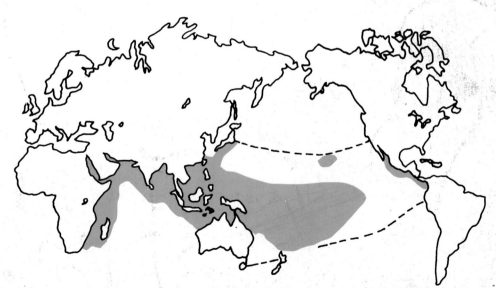

11

# SEA SNAKES

Sea snakes are wonderful divers. Some scientists studied how well sea snakes dive by attaching little radio transmitters to them. When the snakes dived, the transmitters told the scientists how deep they went. One snake dived 150 feet deep. It stayed underwater for more than three and a half hours!

How can sea snakes stay underwater for so long? Sea snakes have a single lung that is larger than the lung of land snakes. They can hold their breaths for a long time. Sea snakes also breathe through their skin. Land snakes can do this only a little bit.

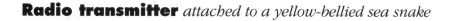

**Radio transmitter** *attached to a yellow-bellied sea snake*

# SEA SNAKES

Living in the ocean takes more than just getting enough oxygen. A big problem for sea snakes is keeping salt out of their bodies. Sea snake blood—like the blood of other animals—has some salt in it. But too much salt can kill any animal, and the ocean is very salty. How does a sea snake keep all of this salt from harming it? Sea snakes solve the salt problem in two ways. They have special skin that keeps out most salt but allows water and gases to pass through. Sea snakes also have a salt gland beneath their tongue. This gland collects any extra salt from the snake's blood.

Each time a sea snake flicks out its tongue, it pushes salt back into the ocean.

*To **live in water,** sea snakes must be different from land snakes in other ways, too.*

Special valves *in their* **noses** *can close tightly to keep water from shooting into their nostrils when they dive.*

To help the snakes swim, their **tails** are shaped like **oars** on a rowboat.

# SEA SNAKES

One more difference between sea and land snakes is that most sea snakes do not have large scales on their bellies. Large belly scales—called scutes—help land snakes grip the ground as they crawl. But in the water, scutes would only slow down a snake. Because sea snakes have only small belly scales, most of them are helpless on land.

An exception are the sea kraits. Unlike the other sea snakes, sea kraits sometimes come ashore. They have medium-sized scutes to help them crawl.

Sea snakes are among the most venomous animals in the world. Their venom has many of the same chemicals as cobra venom. This is not surprising since sea snakes are closely related to cobras. Like other venomous snakes, sea snakes use their venom mostly to kill their prey. The venom also helps some sea snakes protect themselves from predators.

# SEA SNAKES

**More Venomous**     **Sea snake venom strengths**

*Yellow-bellied sea snake*

*Mojave rattlesnake*

*King cobra*

**Less Venomous**

# SEA SNAKES

Some sea snakes eat fish eggs. Some eat squid and cuttlefish.

But mostly sea snakes eat fish. Different sea snakes catch fish in different ways. Some just swim along the bottom until they run into a fish.

Others go poking about in cracks and crevices. When a sea snake finds a fish, it strikes and injects its venom. Then it waits for the fish to die.

**Favorite sea snake snacks**

Being so venomous is a good thing for sea snakes because they must kill their prey **quickly.** Like land snakes, sea snakes swallow their prey whole. A fish that is thrashing around could escape or hurt a sea snake. Fish have sharp spines and teeth. If a fish were still moving while a sea snake was swallowing it, its spines could **poke a hole** in the snake's stomach.

# SEA SNAKES

Even though they are extremely venomous, most sea snakes are not aggressive. Unless they feel threatened, sea snakes rarely attack humans. Some sea snake bites occur when fishermen accidentally catch the snakes in their nets. In most parts of the world when a fisherman catches a sea snake, he picks it up by the tail and throws it back into the water. But sometimes a fisherman accidentally steps on a sea snake. Then he may get bitten. Fishermen don't often die from sea snake bites, however. Sea snakes bite several hundred people each year. But even when they bite to defend themselves, sea snakes do not always inject their venom. If they do, antivenoms are available.

*Some **sea snakes** are so **gentle** that people catch them with their bare hands.*

# SEA SNAKES

The most widely distributed sea snake is the yellow-bellied sea snake, shown in the picture at the left. Scientists believe it is probably the most widely distributed snake of *any* kind. Yellow-bellied sea snakes live in the Pacific and Indian oceans, from Panama all the way to Africa.

The yellow-bellied sea snake is the only snake that can live and breed far out at sea. People have seen these snakes hundreds of miles from land floating on the ocean surface.

Like other true sea snakes, yellow-bellied sea snakes give birth to live babies right in the water.

*Sea snake litters range from 2 to 20 babies. The* **babies** *range in size from 4 to 9 inches.*

# SEA SNAKES

People often find yellow-bellied sea snakes in ocean slicks. Slicks are places where wind and ocean currents have pushed together such floating objects as seaweed and driftwood. Like the seaweed, sea snakes are carried to the slicks. Hundreds, sometimes thousands, of snakes will collect in slicks. Other animals gather there, too. In slicks, it is easy for a sea snake to find food.

Yellow-bellied sea snakes don't hunt fish the same way other sea snakes do. Instead, they wait for fish to come to them. Fish like to hang out under floating objects, where they can find protection from birds and other fish. But when a fish comes near a yellow-bellied sea snake, it doesn't find protection. It becomes a sea snake snack!

*In **1932** a man named **W.P. Lowe** saw a slick of sea snakes more than sixty miles long! It contained **millions** of sea snakes.*

# SEA SNAKES

Yellow-bellied sea snakes are the only sea snakes to reach the Americas. Scientists think that the snakes drifted from Asia to America in Pacific Ocean currents. In the Americas, yellow-bellied sea snakes are common, and live from Ecuador to Baja California. Sometimes warm, tropical waters drift northward to California. When that happens, California beachgoers may be surprised to find yellow-bellied sea snakes washed up next to them. These yellow-bellied sunbathers aren't about to take over California beaches, though. California is far too cold.

*Yellow-bellied sea snakes have no known natural* **enemies**. *Their vivid yellow and black colors send out a signal that says "Don't Eat Me. I Am Poisonous."*
   **Tiger sharks** *and* **sea eagles** *eat other kinds of sea snakes. But most animals know to stay away.*

# SEA SNAKES

People tell fantastic stories about sea snakes. One story from Asia concerns a very poisonous sea snake that lives in deep water. Some fishermen say that if this snake bites a boat, all the people in the boat will die. Another story says that just talking about a sea snake will make it bite you. Like other myths, stories like these are not true.

In some countries people catch sea snakes for profit. In the Philippines, fishing for sea snakes is common. Sea kraits are often captured in cool caves where they come ashore.

Out in the ocean, men attract sea kraits and other sea snakes by "chumming"— throwing dead fish into the water. When enough snakes have gathered around the boat, divers jump overboard. Sea kraits are so gentle that they are easily caught by hand. Divers must be more careful when catching other kinds of sea snakes.

Once they are caught and killed, sea snakes are skinned and cleaned. The meat is fed to pigs and poultry. Sometimes it is cooked and eaten by humans. Sea snake venom is used for scientific research. In China, other parts of the snake are used in medicine.

But the most prized part of the sea snake is its beautiful skin. Many sea snake skins are shipped to Japan. There they are made into belts and other garments. So many sea snakes have been caught and killed that they are now rare in parts of the Philippines.

*Scientists use sea snake* **venoms** *for studying how nerves and muscles work. Sea snake venom is difficult—and* **dangerous**—*to obtain. Biological supply companies sell it for up to $300,000 an ounce!*

# SEA SNAKES

Sea snakes continue to thrive in most other places. At least twenty-seven other kinds of sea snake species live in Southeast Asia. Many more live in Australia and New Guinea. In both these regions, shallow seas and coral reefs like the Great Barrier Reef provide plenty of homes and food for the snakes. Australia has passed laws to protect its sea snakes.

Usually, sea snakes leave people alone. But some sea snakes are very curious. If you're swimming in the tropics, a sea snake may approach you for a closer look. If

that happens, try to swim slowly away from the snake without bumping it. If the snake follows you, stay calm. Don't make any sudden movements. The snake may rub against you or wrap around you, but it most likely won't bite unless you try to handle it. After a few seconds, the snake will probably swim away. Then you will have a sea serpent tale of your very own to tell.

# INDEX

# PHOTO CREDITS

A grateful acknowledgment for the following permissions: Dr. William Dunson (7 top, 20, 30); Carl C. Hansen/ Smithsonian Tropical Research Institute (12, 22); Dr. Harold Heatwole (25); Dr. Harvey Lillywhite (23); Dr. Sherman Minton (6, 7 bottom, 21); Carl W. Roessler (4, 5, 8, 10, 27, 28, 31).

# SPECIAL THANKS TO:

William Dunson, Jeffrey Graham, Harold Heatwole, Harold Voris, Sherman·Minton, and Harvey Lillywhite for their generous assistance.